brownies

easy and delicious recipes

This edition published in 2010
LOVE FOOD is an imprint of Parragon Books Ltd

Parragon
Queen Street House
4 Queen Street
Bath BA1 1HE, UK

Designed by Fiona Roberts
Photography by Bob Wheeler
Home Economy by Val Barrett and Sandra Baddeley
Additional recipes and text by Christine France

ISBN: 978-1-4454-0671-8

Printed in China

Notes for the Reader
This book uses imperial, metric, or US cup measurements. Follow the same
units of measurements throughout, do not mix imperial and metric. All spoon
measurements are level: teaspoons are assumed to be 5ml, and tablespoons are
assumed to be 15ml. Unless otherwise stated, milk is assumed to be low fat and
eggs are medium. The times given are an approximate guide only.

Some recipes contain nuts. If you are allergic to nuts you should avoid
using them and any products containing nuts. Recipes using raw or very
lightly cooked eggs should be avoided by infants, the elderly, pregnant
women, convalescents, and anyone suffering from illness.

Contents

Baking Basics

Ingredients for Success

Sugars The type of sugar you use depends on what the individual recipe calls for. Use superfine sugar where a recipe doesn't specify a particular type, as this is the best for most cakes. Golden superfine sugar is useful for adding color to paler mixtures, and is usually less refined than white superfine. Brown and molasses sugars are less refined, so they have a coating of molasses and are used to add a richness of flavor and give a golden or deeper brown color. Soft light or dark brown sugars are refined sugar, colored and flavored, and can replace molasses sugar.

Granulated sugar has larger crystals, so it can leave speckles in some mixtures. But, if you run out of superfine, you can grind granulated in a food processor for a few seconds as a substitute. Turbinado is fine for melting methods, and to sprinkle for a sweet crunchy topping. Confectioners' sugar is best kept for frostings and sprinkling, as it gives a heavy result in cake mixtures. Finally, honey, light corn syrup, and maple syrup can in some recipes replace part of the sugar, but may give a heavier result. But, as they have a sweeter taste, you can use about a fourth less than sugar. They're great for drizzling, too, either on warm brownies straight from the oven or glazing when cooled, for a lovely glossy top and rich flavor.

Flours All-purpose white flour is the usual choice for brownies, but some recipes may state self-rising flour, which has an added rising agent. If you don't have self-rising flour, add $2^1/2$ tsp baking powder to all-purpose flour and sift together to make self-rising.

Fats Most brownie recipes use butter, which is best for flavor, but you can also use a good quality hard block margarine instead. Soft tub margarines should be used only where the recipe calls for them, as these need a slightly different method. Low-fat spreads cannot be used in most ordinary recipes, as they have a high water content. Light-flavored oils, such as sunflower, can be used in some mixtures, particularly those with a melting method, but remember that they have the same fat content as butter.

Eggs Unless your recipe states otherwise, the eggs should be large. For most mixtures, it's best to use eggs at room temperature, as they will hold more air than chilled ones.

Choosing Chocolate Not all brownies are chocolate, but the most classic ones are chocolate-rich, and depend on good chocolate for their flavor and texture. There's a bewildering array of types of chocolate to choose from, so you need to choose carefully.

To put it simply, chocolate is made up of cocoa solids, cocoa butter, and sugar, sometimes with the addition of vanilla, vegetable fat, and milk solids. Semisweet or bittersweet chocolate must contain a minimum of 34% cocoa solids, and as an approximate guide, the higher the cocoa solids content, the better the flavor.

So, check out the label before you buy—for the recipes in this book, we recommend using chocolate with at least 60% cocoa solids, and ardent chocoholics will prefer to go for one with at least 70% cocoa solids for that intense kick of bittersweet chocolate.

Techniques and Tips for Top Brownies

Preheating   It's always best to preheat the oven for 10–15 minutes before baking, as you'll need a hot oven to achieve a good texture. Adjust the shelves to the position you need before turning on the oven; unless otherwise stated, the brownies should be baked on a middle shelf in a conventional oven.

Preparing pans   Depending on the mixture, you will need to grease, grease and line, or grease and flour the pan, so the brownies turn out easily.

Use a light-flavored oil or melted butter for greasing and brush it over the base and sides of the pan with a pastry brush.

Use baking parchment for lining pans, as this peels off easily. For brownies and traybakes, you usually need to line only the base of pans. To do this, place the pan on the parchment and use a pencil to draw around the base of the pan. With scissors, cut just inside the outline of the shape drawn, and the cut parchment should fit the pan neatly.

If a recipe says you should grease and flour the pan, simply brush with oil or melted butter as above, then sprinkle a little all-purpose flour into the pan. Shake the pan, tipping the flour to coat the base and sides, then tip out the excess.

Techniques for Success

Melting and creaming methods are the ones used most for brownies, and the melting method is the easiest. The fat, sugar, and often chocolate are melted together first in a pan. Keep the heat low, as boiling will spoil the flavor. Remove from the heat and stir in the eggs and dry ingredients, but don't overmix. Work quickly to get the mixture into the oven straight away, as rising agents can start to react as soon as the ingredients are mixed.

The creaming method involves beating together the fat and sugar with a wooden spoon or hand-held mixer until soft, pale, and creamy. Then, the eggs should be beaten in gradually—if they're added too fast, the mixture may curdle—and the flour and other ingredients can then be lightly "folded" in, preferably with a metal spoon, to keep in as much air as possible.

sweet indulgence

the classics

chocolate brownies

makes 15

8 oz/225 g butter, diced,
plus extra for greasing

5¹/2 oz/150 g dark chocolate,
chopped

1¹/2 cups all-purpose flour

1 cup dark muscovado sugar

4 eggs, beaten

¹/4 cup blanched hazelnuts,
chopped

¹/2 cup golden raisins

¹/2 cup dark chocolate chips

4 oz/115 g white chocolate,
melted, to decorate

Preheat the oven to 350°F/180°C. Grease and line an 11 x 7-inch/28 x 18-cm rectangular cake pan with baking parchment.

Put the butter and chopped dark chocolate into a heatproof bowl and set over a pan of simmering water until melted. Remove from the heat. Sift the flour into a large bowl, add the sugar, and mix well. Stir the eggs into the chocolate mixture, then beat into the flour mixture. Add the nuts, golden raisins, and chocolate chips and mix well. Spoon evenly into the cake pan and level the surface.

Bake in the oven for 30 minutes, or until firm. To check whether the cake is cooked through, insert a skewer into the center—it should come out clean. If not, return the cake to the oven for a few minutes. Remove from the oven and let cool for 15 minutes. Turn out onto a wire rack to cool completely. To decorate, drizzle the melted white chocolate in fine lines over the cake, then cut into bars or squares. Let set before serving.

chocolate fudge brownies

makes 16

3 oz/85 g butter, plus extra
for greasing
scant 1 cup lowfat soft cheese
1/2 tsp vanilla extract
generous 1 cup superfine sugar
2 eggs
3 tbsp unsweetened cocoa
3/4 cup self-rising flour, sifted
1/3 cup chopped pecans

fudge frosting

4 tbsp butter
1 tbsp milk
2/3 cup confectioners' sugar
2 tbsp unsweetened cocoa
pecans, to decorate (optional)

Preheat the oven to 350°F/180°C. Lightly grease an 8-inch/20-cm square shallow cake pan and line the bottom with baking parchment.

Beat together the cheese, vanilla extract, and 5 teaspoons of superfine sugar until smooth, then set aside.

Beat the eggs and remaining superfine sugar together until light and fluffy. Place the butter and unsweetened cocoa in a small pan and heat gently, stirring until the butter melts and the mixture combines, then stir it into the egg mixture. Fold in the flour and nuts.

Pour half of the cake batter into the pan and smooth the top. Carefully spread the soft cheese over it, then cover it with the remaining cake batter. Bake in the preheated oven for 40–45 minutes. Let cool in the pan.

To make the frosting, melt the butter in the milk. Stir in the confectioners' sugar and unsweetened cocoa. Spread the frosting over the brownies and decorate with pecans (if using). Let the frosting set, then cut into squares to serve.

pecan brownies

makes 20

8 oz/225 g unsalted butter,
plus extra for greasing

2¹/2 oz/70 g semisweet chocolate

scant 1 cup all-purpose flour

³/4 tsp baking soda

¹/4 tsp baking powder

¹/3 cup pecans

¹/2 cup raw sugar,
plus extra for decorating

¹/2 tsp almond extract

1 egg

1 tsp milk

Preheat the oven to 350°F/180°C. Grease a large cookie sheet and line it with baking parchment.

Put the chocolate in a heatproof bowl set over a pan of gently simmering water and heat until it is melted. Meanwhile, sift together the flour, baking soda, and baking powder in a large bowl.

Finely chop the pecans and set aside. In a separate bowl, cream together the butter and sugar, then mix in the almond extract and the egg. Remove the chocolate from the heat and stir into the butter mixture. Add the flour mixture, milk, and chopped nuts to the bowl and stir until well combined.

Spoon the dough onto the greased sheet and smooth it. Transfer to the preheated oven and cook for 30 minutes, or until firm to the touch (it should still be a little soft in the center). Remove from the oven and let cool completely. Sprinkle with sugar, cut into 20 squares, and serve.

double chocolate brownies

makes 9 large or 16 small
4 oz/115 g butter, plus extra
for greasing
4 oz/115 g semisweet chocolate,
broken into pieces
1 1/3 cups golden superfine sugar
pinch of salt
1 tsp vanilla extract
2 large eggs
1 cup all-purpose flour
2 tbsp unsweetened cocoa
1/2 cup white chocolate chips

fudge sauce
4 tbsp butter
generous 1 cup golden
superfine sugar
2/3 cup milk
generous 1 cup heavy cream
2/3 cup corn syrup
7 oz/200 g semisweet chocolate,
broken into pieces

Preheat the oven to 350°F/180°C. Grease and line the bottom of a 7-inch/18-cm square cake pan with baking parchment. Place the butter and chocolate in a small heatproof bowl set over a saucepan of gently simmering water until melted. Stir until smooth. Let cool slightly. Stir in the sugar, salt, and vanilla extract. Add the eggs, one at a time, stirring well, until blended.

Sift the flour and unsweetened cocoa into the cake batter and beat until smooth. Stir in the chocolate chips, then pour the batter into the pan. Bake in the preheated oven for 35–40 minutes, or until the top is evenly colored and a skewer inserted into the center comes out almost clean. Let cool slightly while preparing the sauce.

To make the sauce, place the butter, sugar, milk, cream, and syrup in a small saucepan and heat gently until the sugar has dissolved. Bring to a boil and stir for 10 minutes, or until the mixture is caramel-colored. Remove from the heat and add the chocolate. Stir until smooth. Cut the brownies into squares and serve immediately with the sauce.

sticky chocolate brownies

makes 9

3 oz/85 g unsalted butter,
plus extra for greasing

$^3/_4$ cup superfine sugar

$^1/_2$ cup dark brown sugar

4$^1/_2$ oz/125 g semisweet
chocolate

1 tbsp corn syrup

2 eggs

1 tsp chocolate or vanilla extract

$^3/_4$ cup all-purpose flour

2 tbsp unsweetened cocoa,
plus extra to dust

$^1/_2$ tsp baking powder

Preheat the oven to 350°F/180°C. Lightly grease an 8-inch/20-cm shallow square cake pan and line the bottom with baking parchment.

Place the butter, sugars, chocolate, and corn syrup in a heavy-bottomed saucepan and heat gently, stirring until the mixture is well blended and smooth. Remove from the heat and let cool.

Beat together the eggs and chocolate or vanilla extract. Whisk in the cooled chocolate mixture.

Sift together the flour, unsweetened cocoa, and baking powder and fold carefully into the egg and chocolate mixture using a metal spoon or spatula.

Spoon the cake batter into the prepared pan and bake in the preheated oven for 25 minutes, until the top is crisp and the edge of the cake is starting to shrink away from the pan. The inside of the cake batter will still be quite stodgy and soft to the touch.

Let the cake cool completely in the pan, dust with unsweetened cocoa powder, then cut into squares and serve.

white chocolate brownies

makes 9

4 oz/115 g butter, plus extra
for greasing

8 oz/225 g white chocolate

2/3 cup walnut pieces

2 eggs

1 cup brown sugar

1 cup self-rising flour

Preheat the oven to 350°F/180°C. Lightly grease a 7-inch/18-cm square cake pan.

Coarsely chop 6 oz/175 g of the chocolate and all the walnuts. Put the remaining chocolate and the butter in a heatproof bowl, set over a pan of gently simmering water. When melted, stir together, then set aside to cool slightly.

Whisk the eggs and sugar together, then beat in the cooled chocolate mixture until well mixed. Fold in the flour, chopped chocolate, and the walnuts. Turn the mixture into the prepared pan and smooth the surface.

Transfer the pan to the preheated oven and bake the brownies for about 30 minutes, until just set. The mixture should still be a little soft in the center. Let cool in the pan, then cut into 9 squares before serving.

chocolate chip brownies

makes 12

8 oz/225 g butter, softened,
plus extra for greasing
5$^{1}/_{2}$ oz/150 g
semisweet chocolate,
broken into pieces
2 cups self-rising flour
$^{1}/_{2}$ cup superfine sugar
4 eggs, beaten
$^{1}/_{2}$ cup chopped pistachios
3$^{1}/_{2}$ oz/100 g white chocolate,
chopped coarsely
confectioners' sugar,
for dusting (optional)

Preheat the oven to 350°F/180°C. Lightly grease a 9-inch/23-cm baking pan and line with baking parchment.

Melt the semisweet chocolate and butter in a heatproof bowl set over a pan of gently simmering water. Let cool slightly.

Sift the flour into a separate mixing bowl and stir in the superfine sugar.

Stir the eggs into the melted chocolate mixture, then pour this mixture into the flour and sugar mixture, beating well. Stir in the pistachios and white chocolate, then pour the cake batter into the pan, spreading it evenly into the corners.

Bake in the preheated oven for 30–35 minutes, until firm to the touch. Let cool in the pan for 20 minutes, then turn out onto a wire rack.

Let cool completely, then cut into 12 pieces and dust with confectioners' sugar if liked.

cappuccino brownies

makes 15

8 oz/225 g butter, softened, plus
extra for greasing
generous 1¹/2 cups self-rising flour
1 tsp baking powder
1 tsp unsweetened cocoa,
plus extra for dusting
generous 1 cup golden
superfine sugar
4 eggs, beaten
3 tbsp instant coffee powder,
dissolved in 2 tbsp hot water

fudge frosting
4 oz/115 g white chocolate,
broken into pieces
2 oz/55 g butter, softened
3 tbsp milk
1³/4 cups confectioners' sugar

Preheat the oven to 350°F/180°C. Grease and line the bottom of a shallow 11 x 7-inch/ 28 x 18-cm pan with baking parchment. Sift the flour, baking powder, and cocoa into a bowl and add the butter, superfine sugar, eggs, and coffee. Beat well, by hand or with an electric whisk, until smooth, then spoon into the pan and smooth the top.

Bake in the oven for 35–40 minutes, or until risen and firm. Let cool in the pan for 10 minutes, then turn out onto a wire rack and peel off the lining paper. Let cool completely. To make the frosting, place the chocolate, butter, and milk in a bowl set over a pan of simmering water and stir until the chocolate has melted.

Remove the bowl from the pan and sift in the confectioners' sugar. Beat until smooth, then spread over the cake. Dust the top of the cake with sifted cocoa, then cut into squares.

mocha brownies

makes 16

2 oz/55 g butter, plus extra
for greasing
4 oz/115 g semisweet chocolate,
broken into pieces
scant 1 cup brown sugar
2 eggs
1 tbsp instant coffee powder
dissolved in 1 tbsp
hot water, cooled
scant 2/3 cup all-purpose flour
1/2 tsp baking powder
1/3 cup coarsely chopped pecans

decoration
1 cup confectioners' sugar
1–2 tbsp water
chopped pecans

Preheat the oven to 350°F/180°C. Grease and line the bottom of an 8-inch/20-cm square cake pan with baking parchment. Place the chocolate and butter in a heavy-bottomed pan over low heat until melted. Stir and let cool.

Place the sugar and eggs in a large bowl and cream together until light and fluffy. Fold in the chocolate mixture and cooled coffee and mix thoroughly. Sift in the flour and baking powder and lightly fold into the mixture, then carefully fold in the pecans.

Pour the batter into the prepared pan and bake in the preheated oven for 25–30 minutes, or until firm and a skewer inserted into the center comes out clean.

Let cool in the pan for a few minutes, then run a knife round the edge of the cake to loosen it. Turn the cake out onto a wire rack and peel off the lining paper. Let cool completely. When cold, cut into squares.

Mix the confectioners' sugar with the water to give a coating consistency. Trickle over or around each brownie and sprinkle with chopped pecans.

ginger chocolate chip brownies

makes 15

4 pieces preserved ginger in syrup
1 1/2 cups all-purpose flour
1 1/2 tsp ground ginger
1 tsp ground cinnamon
1/4 tsp ground cloves
1/4 tsp grated nutmeg
1/2 cup brown sugar
4 oz/115 g butter
1/3 cup corn syrup
1/2 cup semisweet chocolate chips

Preheat the oven to 300°F/150°C. Finely chop the preserved ginger. Sift the flour, ground ginger, cinnamon, cloves, and nutmeg into a large bowl. Stir in the chopped preserved ginger and sugar.

Put the butter and the syrup in a pan and heat gently until melted. Bring to a boil, then pour the mixture into the flour mixture, stirring all the time. Beat until the mixture is cool enough to handle.

Add the chocolate chips to the mixture. Press evenly into a 12 x 8-inch/30 x 20-cm jelly roll pan.

Bake in the oven for 30 minutes. Cut into fingers, then let cool in the pan.

super mocha brownies

makes 12

5¹/₂ oz/150 g good-quality
semisweet chocolate (70 %
cocoa solids)
3¹/₂ oz/100 g dairy-free margarine,
plus extra for greasing
1 tsp strong instant coffee
1 tsp vanilla extract
1 cup ground almonds
scant 1 cup superfine sugar
4 eggs, separated
confectioners' sugar,
to decorate (optional)

Preheat the oven to 350°F/180°C. Grease an 8-inch/20-cm square cake pan and line the bottom with baking parchment.

Melt the chocolate and margarine in a heatproof bowl placed over a pan of gently simmering water, making sure that the bottom of the bowl does not touch the water. Stir very occasionally until the chocolate and margarine have melted and are smooth.

Carefully remove the bowl from the heat. Let cool slightly, then stir in the coffee and vanilla extract. Add the almonds and sugar and mix well until combined. Lightly beat the egg yolks in a separate bowl, then stir into the chocolate mixture.

Whisk the egg whites in a large bowl until they form stiff peaks. Gently fold a large spoonful of the egg whites into the chocolate mixture, then fold in the remainder until completely incorporated.

Spoon the mixture into the prepared pan and bake in the preheated oven for 35–40 minutes, or until risen and firm on top but still slightly gooey in the center. Let cool in the pan, then turn out, remove the lining paper, and cut into 12 pieces. Dust with confectioners' sugar before serving, if liked.

naughty but nice

new twists

sour cream brownies

makes 9 large or 16 small

2 oz/55 g butter, plus extra
for greasing
4 oz/115 g semisweet chocolate,
broken into pieces
3/4 cup dark brown sugar
2 eggs
2 tbsp strong coffee, cooled
generous 1/2 cup all-purpose flour
1/2 tsp baking powder
pinch of salt
1/4 cup shelled walnuts, chopped

frosting

4 oz/115 g semisweet chocolate,
broken into pieces
2/3 cup sour cream
mini chocolate balls, to decorate

Preheat the oven to 350°F/180°C. Grease an 8-inch/20-cm square cake pan with butter and line with baking parchment. Place the chocolate and butter in a small heatproof bowl and set over a saucepan of gently simmering water until melted. Stir until smooth. Remove from the heat and let cool.

Beat the sugar and eggs together until pale and thick. Fold in the chocolate mixture and coffee. Mix well. Sift the flour, baking powder, and salt into the cake batter and fold in. Fold in the walnuts. Pour the cake batter into the pan and bake in the oven for 20–25 minutes, or until set. Let cool in the pan.

To make the frosting, melt the chocolate in a heatproof bowl set over a saucepan of gently simmering water until melted. Stir in the sour cream and beat until evenly blended. Spoon the topping over the brownies and make a swirling pattern with a spatula. Let set in a cool place. Cut into bars or squares, then remove from the pan and serve, decorated with mini chocolate balls if liked.

walnut & cinnamon blondies

makes 9

4 oz/115 g butter, plus extra for greasing

generous 1 cup brown sugar

1 egg

1 egg yolk

1 cup self-rising flour

1 tsp ground cinnamon

generous 1/2 cup coarsely chopped walnuts

Preheat the oven to 350°F/180°C. Grease and line the bottom of a 7-inch/18-cm square cake pan with baking parchment. Place the butter and sugar in a pan over low heat and stir until the sugar has dissolved. Cook, stirring, for an additional 1 minute. The mixture will bubble slightly, but do not let it boil. Let cool for 10 minutes.

Stir the egg and egg yolk into the mixture. Sift in the flour and cinnamon, add the nuts, and stir until just blended. Pour the cake batter into the prepared pan, then bake in the oven for 20–25 minutes, or until springy in the center and a skewer inserted into the center of the cake comes out clean.

Let cool in the pan for a few minutes, then run a knife around the edge of the cake to loosen it. Turn the cake out onto a wire rack and peel off the paper.

Let cool completely. When cold, cut into squares.

upside-down toffee apple brownies

makes 8–10

toffee apple topping
generous 1/3 cup light
brown sugar
2 oz/55 g unsalted butter
1 eating apple, cored and
thinly sliced

brownies
4 oz/115 g unsalted butter
3/4 cup light brown sugar
2 eggs, beaten
13/4 cups all-purpose flour
1 tsp baking powder
1/2 tsp baking soda
11/2 tsp apple pie spice
2 eating apples, peeled and
coarsely grated
3/4 cup chopped hazelnuts

Preheat the oven to 350°F/180°C. Grease a 9-inch/23-cm square shallow cake pan.

For the topping, place the sugar and butter in a small pan and heat gently, stirring, until melted. Pour into the prepared cake pan. Arrange the apple slices on top.

For the brownies, place the butter and sugar in a bowl and beat well until pale and fluffy. Gradually beat in the eggs.

Sift together the flour, baking powder, baking soda, and spice and fold into the mixture. Stir in the apples and nuts.

Pour into the cake pan and bake for 35–40 minutes, until firm and golden. Cool in the pan for 10 minutes, then turn out upside down, and cut into squares.

rocky road brownies

makes 16

scant 1 cup all-purpose flour

scant 3/4 cup superfine sugar

3 tbsp unsweetened cocoa

1/2 tsp baking powder

8 oz/22 g butter, melted

2 eggs, beaten

1 tsp vanilla extract

1/3 cup candied cherries,
cut into fourths

2/3 cup blanched almonds,
chopped

fudge frosting

1 3/4 cups confectioners' sugar

2 tbsp unsweetened cocoa

3 tbsp evaporated milk

1/2 tsp vanilla extract

generous 1 cup chopped
marshmallows

Preheat the oven to 325°F/160°C. Grease a 9-inch/23-cm square, shallow cake pan and sprinkle lightly with flour.

Sift together the flour, sugar, cocoa, and baking powder and make a well in the center. Stir in the melted butter, eggs, and vanilla extract and beat well to mix thoroughly.

Stir in the cherries and almonds. Pour into the prepared pan and bake for 35–40 minutes, until just firm on top. Leave to cool in the pan.

Meanwhile, make the frosting. Place all the ingredients in a large bowl and beat well to mix to a smooth, just spreading consistency.

Spread the cooled brownies with the frosting, swirling lightly, and sprinkle with marshmallows. Let stand until the frosting sets, then cut into squares.

rich apricot blondies

makes 12

12 oz/350 g white chocolate
3 oz/85 g unsalted butter
1 tsp vanilla extract
3 eggs, beaten
2/3 cup light brown sugar
1 cup self-rising flour
3/4 cup coarsely chopped
macadamia nuts
scant 1/2 cup ready-to-eat dried
apricots, coarsely chopped

Preheat the oven to 375°F/190°C. Lightly grease an 11 x 7-inch/28 x 18-cm pan and line the bottom with baking parchment.

Chop half the chocolate into small chunks. Melt the remaining chocolate with the butter in a small pan over very low heat and stir until melted. Remove from the heat and stir in the vanilla extract.

Whisk the eggs and sugar together in a large bowl until pale. Beat in the melted chocolate mixture. Fold in the flour evenly, then stir in the macadamia nuts, apricots, and chopped chocolate.

Spoon into the prepared pan and smooth the top level. Bake for 25–30 minutes, or until firm and golden brown.

Leave to cool in the pan. Turn out when cold and cut into squares or triangles.

pecan brownie muffins

makes 12

1 cup pecans

scant 1 cup all-purpose flour

generous 3/4 cup superfine sugar

1/4 tsp salt

1 tbsp baking powder

8 oz/225 g unsalted butter

4 oz/115 g semisweet chocolate, broken into pieces

4 eggs, beaten

1 tsp vanilla extract

Preheat the oven to 400°F/200°F. Place paper muffin cases in a 12-cup muffin pan. Reserve 12 pecan halves and coarsely chop the rest.

Sift the flour, sugar, salt, and baking powder into a large bowl and make a well in the center. Melt the butter and chocolate in a small pan over very low heat, stirring frequently. Add to the flour mixture and stir to mix evenly.

Add the eggs and vanilla extract and mix together just until the ingredients are evenly moistened. Stir in the chopped pecans.

Spoon the batter into the muffin cases, filling each about three-fourths full. Place a pecan half on top of each. Bake for 20–25 minutes, or until well risen and firm to the touch.

marbled choc cheesecake brownies

makes 12

6 oz/170 g unsalted butter

3 tbsp unsweetened cocoa

1 cup golden superfine sugar

2 eggs, beaten

generous 1 cup all-purpose flour

cheesecake mix

generous 1 cup ricotta cheese

3 tbsp golden superfine sugar

1 egg, beaten

Preheat the oven to 350°F/180°C. Grease an 11 x 7-inch/28 x 18-cm cake pan.

Melt the butter in a medium pan, remove from the heat, and stir in the unsweetened cocoa and sugar. Beat in the eggs, then add the flour, and stir to mix evenly. Pour into the prepared pan.

For the cheesecake mix, beat together the ricotta, sugar, and egg, then drop teaspoonfuls of the mixture over the chocolate mixture. Use a metal spatula to swirl the two mixtures lightly together.

Bake for 40–45 minutes, until just firm to the touch. Cool in the pan, then cut into squares or bars.

maple glazed pistachio brownies

makes 16

4 oz/115 g bittersweet chocolate,
broken into pieces
6 oz/170 g unsalted butter
1 1/4 cups superfine sugar
4 eggs, beaten
1 tsp vanilla extract
1 3/4 cups all-purpose flour
3/4 cup shelled pistachio nuts,
skinned and chopped

glaze

4 oz/115 g bittersweet chocolate,
broken into pieces
1/2 cup crème fraîche
2 tbsp maple syrup

Preheat the oven to 375°F/190°C. Lightly grease a 12 x 8-inch/30 x 20-cm shallow cake pan.

Place the chocolate with the butter in a small pan over very low heat and stir until melted. Remove from the heat and stir in the sugar.

Whisk the eggs and vanilla extract together in a large bowl until pale. Beat in the melted chocolate mixture.

Fold in the flour evenly, then stir in half a cup of the pistachios.

Spoon into the prepared pan and smooth the top level. Bake for 25–30 minutes, or until firm and golden brown.

For the glaze, melt the chocolate in a bowl over hot water. Stir in the crème fraîche and maple syrup and beat until smooth and glossy.

Spread the glaze over the brownies evenly with a metal spatula. Sprinkle with the remaining pistachios and let stand until the topping is set. Cut into squares.

cranberry sour cream brownies

makes 12

4 oz/115 g unsalted butter

4 tbsp unsweetened cocoa

scant 1 cup light brown sugar

1 1/4 cups self-rising flour

2 eggs, beaten

1 cup fresh cranberries

for the swirl

2/3 cup sour cream

1 tbsp superfine sugar

1 tbsp self-rising flour

1 egg yolk

1/2 tsp vanilla extract

1 oz/25–30 g semisweet

chocolate, grated (optional)

Preheat the oven to 375°F/190°C. Lightly grease a 12 x 8-inch/30 x 20-cm shallow cake pan and dust lightly with flour.

Place the butter, cocoa, and sugar in a pan and stir over low heat until just melted. Remove from the heat and let cool slightly.

Quickly stir in the flour and eggs, and beat hard until thoroughly mixed to a smooth batter. Stir in the cranberries, then spread the mixture into the prepared pan.

For the swirl, beat together all the ingredients, except the grated chocolate, until smooth, then spoon the mixture over the chocolate batter, swirling evenly with a metal spatula.

Bake for 35–40 minutes, or until risen and firm. Let cool in the pan, then cut into squares. Decorate with grated chocolate if liked.

low fat banana cardamom brownies

makes 16

1 cup all-purpose flour

3 tbsp unsweetened cocoa

2 tbsp nonfat dry milk

$1/4$ tsp baking powder

$1/4$ tsp salt

2 ripe bananas

$2/3$ cups light brown sugar

2 egg whites

generous $2/3$ cup plain lowfat yogurt

seeds from 2 cardamom pods, crushed

shredded coconut, toasted, to sprinkle

Preheat the oven to 350°F/180°C. Grease a 9-inch/23-cm square shallow cake pan.

Sift the flour, unsweetened cocoa, dry milk, baking powder, and salt into a large bowl and make a well in the center.

Mash the bananas and beat with the sugar, egg whites, yogurt, and cardamom seeds. Stir into the dry ingredients, mixing evenly.

Spoon into the prepared pan and bake for 25–30 minutes, or until just firm. Sprinkle with toasted coconut, let cool in the pan, and cut into squares when cold.

carrot streusel brownies

makes 15

1¼ cups light brown sugar

4 oz/115 g unsalted butter, softened

2 eggs, beaten

1 tsp vanilla extract

1½ cups all-purpose flour

½ tsp baking soda

½ tsp baking powder

⅔ cup golden raisins

scant 1 cup finely grated carrots

½ cup chopped walnuts

streusel topping

⅓ cup finely chopped walnuts

3 tbsp molasses sugar

2 tbsp all-purpose flour

½ tsp ground cinnamon

½ oz/15 g unsalted butter, melted

Preheat the oven to 375°F/190°C. Lightly grease a 12 x 8-inch/30 x 20-cm shallow cake pan.

Cream together the sugar and butter until pale. Beat in the eggs and vanilla extract. Sift the flour, baking soda, and baking powder into the mixture and fold in evenly. Stir in the golden raisins, carrots, and walnuts.

Spread the mixture into the prepared pan. Combine all the topping ingredients to make a crumbly mixture and sprinkle evenly over the cake mixture.

Bake for 45–55 minutes, or until golden brown and just firm to the touch. Let cool in the pan, then cut into squares or bars.

pure luxury

made to impress

mint julep brownie cake

makes 6–8

5¹/₂ oz/150 g bittersweet
chocolate, broken into pieces
6 oz/175 g unsalted butter
2 eggs
scant 1 cup molasses sugar
3 tbsp bourbon
1 tbsp chopped fresh mint
generous 1 cup self-rising flour
1 tbsp confectioners' sugar
mint sprigs, to decorate

sauce

4 oz/115 g bittersweet chocolate,
broken into pieces
¹/₂ cup light cream
¹/₄ tsp peppermint extract

Preheat the oven to 350°F/180°C. Grease an 11 x 7-inch/28 x 18-cm cake pan.

Place the chocolate and butter in a pan over very low heat and stir occasionally until melted. Remove from the heat.

Beat together the eggs, molasses sugar, bourbon, and mint, then beat quickly into the chocolate mixture. Fold in the flour and mix evenly.

Pour the mixture into the prepared pan and smooth the surface. Bake for 30–35 minutes, until just firm but still slightly soft inside.

Let cool in the pan for 15 minutes, then remove from the pan, and use a 3-inch cutter to stamp out 6 rounds.

For the chocolate mint sauce, place the chocolate, cream, and peppermint extract in a small pan and heat gently, stirring, until melted and smooth.

To serve, sprinkle with confectioners' sugar, drizzle with the chocolate sauce, and decorate with sprigs of mint.

brownie bottom cheesecake

serves 12

brownie base

4 oz/115g unsalted butter

4 oz/115 g bittersweet chocolate,
broken into pieces

1 cup superfine sugar

2 eggs, beaten

1/4 cup milk

1 cup all-purpose flour

topping

2 1/4 cups cream cheese
or farmer's cheese

2/3 cup golden superfine sugar

3 eggs, beaten

1 tsp vanilla extract

1/2 cup plain yogurt

melted semisweet chocolate,
to drizzle

Preheat the oven to 350°F/180°C. Lightly grease and flour a 9-inch/23-cm springform cake pan.

Melt the butter and chocolate in a pan over low heat, stirring frequently, until smooth. Remove from the heat and beat in the sugar.

Add the eggs and milk, beating well. Stir in the flour, mixing just until blended. Spoon into the prepared pan, spreading evenly.

Bake for 25 minutes. Remove from the oven while preparing the topping. Reduce the oven temperature to 325°F/160°C.

For the topping, beat together the cheese, sugar, eggs, and vanilla extract until well blended. Stir in the yogurt, then pour over the brownie base. Bake for a further 45–55 minutes, or until the center is almost set.

Run a knife around the edge of the cake to loosen from the pan. Let cool before removing from the pan. Chill in the refrigerator for 4 hours or overnight before cutting into slices. Serve drizzled with melted chocolate.

black russian brownies

makes 8–10

4 oz/115 g bittersweet chocolate, broken into pieces

4 oz/115 g unsalted butter

$^1/_2$ tsp coarsely ground black peppercorns

4 eggs, beaten

$1^1/_4$ cups superfine sugar

1 tsp vanilla extract

3 tbsp Kahlua liqueur

2 tbsp vodka

$1^1/_3$ cups all-purpose flour

$^1/_4$ tsp baking powder

$^1/_2$ cup chopped walnuts

kahlua cream topping

scant 1 cup crème fraîche

2 tbsp Kahlua liqueur

unsweetened cocoa, to sprinkle

Preheat the oven to 350°F/180°C. Grease and line the base of a 12 x 8-inch/30 x 20-cm shallow cake pan with baking parchment.

Melt the chocolate and butter with the peppercorns in a small pan over low heat. Remove from the heat and let cool slightly.

Beat together the eggs, sugar, and vanilla extract in a large bowl and stir in the chocolate mixture, Kahlua, and vodka.

Sift the flour and baking powder and stir evenly into the chocolate mixture. Stir in the walnuts. Pour into the pan and bake for 20–25 minutes, until just firm to the touch.

Let cool for a few minutes, then cut into squares, and lift carefully from the pan onto serving plates.

For the topping, stir the Kahlua into the crème fraîche and spoon a generous mound on each serving of brownie. Sprinkle with a little unsweetened cocoa and serve immediately.

mochachino brownies with white mocha sauce

makes 8–9

4 oz/115 g unsalted butter

4 oz/115 g bittersweet chocolate, broken into pieces

2 tbsp strong black coffee

1¼ cups golden superfine sugar

3 eggs, beaten

¾ cup all-purpose flour

⅓ cup milk chocolate chips

½ cup toasted walnuts, skinned and chopped

walnuts, to decorate

sauce

scant ½ cup heavy cream

3 oz/85 g white chocolate, broken into pieces

1 tbsp strong black coffee

Preheat the oven to 350°F/180°C. Grease and line a 9-inch/23-cm square cake pan with baking parchment.

Place the butter, chocolate, and coffee in a pan over low heat and stir until just melted and smooth. Let cool slightly.

Whisk in the superfine sugar and eggs. Beat in the flour, chocolate chips, and walnuts. Pour into the prepared pan.

Bake for 30–35 minutes, until just firm but still moist inside. Let cool in the pan, then cut into squares or bars.

Meanwhile, make the sauce by placing all the ingredients in a small pan over low heat, stirring occasionally, until melted and smooth.

Place the brownies on individual plates and spoon the warm sauce over the top. Decorate with the walnuts.

blonde brownie hearts with raspberry sauce

makes 8

4 oz/115 g white chocolate,
broken into pieces

4 oz/115 g unsalted butter

2 eggs, beaten

3/4 cup superfine sugar

seeds from 1 vanilla bean

1 1/4 cups all-purpose flour

8 small squares
bittersweet chocolate

whipped cream, to serve (optional)

raspberry sauce

1 1/2 cups raspberries,
thawed if frozen

2 tbsp amaretto liqueur

1 tbsp confectioners' sugar

Preheat the oven to 350°F/180°C. Oil and lightly flour 8 individual heart-shaped baking pans, each 2/3-cup capacity.

Place the chocolate and butter in a pan over low heat and heat gently, stirring, until just melted. Remove from the heat.

Whisk together the eggs, sugar, and vanilla seeds until smooth and thick. Lightly fold in the flour, then stir in the chocolate mixture, and mix evenly.

Pour the batter into the pans, adding a square of chocolate to the center of each, without pressing down. Bake for 20–25 minutes, until just firm. Let stand in the pans for 5 minutes.

Meanwhile, purée half the raspberries with the amaretto and confectioners' sugar, then rub through a strainer to remove the seeds.

Run a knife around the edge of each heart to loosen from the pan and turn out onto individual plates. Spoon the raspberry sauce around, decorate with the remaining raspberries, and serve warm, with whipped cream, if liked.

black forest brownies

makes 8

3/4 cup all-purpose flour
1/2 tsp baking powder
4 oz/115 g unsalted butter
1/2 cup unsweetened cocoa
2 eggs, beaten
generous 3/4 cup superfine sugar
1 tsp vanilla extract
1/2 tsp almond extract
scant 1 cup pitted dark cherries, cut into fourths
chocolate curls and whole cherries, to decorate

topping

2/3 cup heavy or whipping cream
1 tbsp Kirsch liqueur

Preheat the oven to 350°F/180°C. Grease an 11 x 7-inch/28 x 18-cm shallow cake pan.

Sift together the flour and baking powder.

Melt the butter in a large pan over medium heat. Remove from the heat and add the unsweetened cocoa, stirring until smooth. Beat in the eggs, sugar, vanilla, and almond extract.

Fold in the flour and cherries. Pour into the prepared pan and bake for 25–30 minutes, or until just firm to the touch. Let cool slightly in the pan.

Cut into squares and remove from the pan. Whip the cream with the Kirsch and spoon a little onto each brownie. Decorate with chocolate curls and serve with extra cherries.

rich ginger brownies with port cream

serves 8

7 oz/200 g bittersweet chocolate, broken into pieces

6 oz/170 g unsalted butter

1 cup sugar

4 eggs, beaten

2 tsp vanilla extract

1 tbsp preserved ginger syrup

generous ³/4 cup all-purpose flour

¹/4 cup chopped preserved ginger

2 tbsp chopped candied ginger, to decorate

port cream

scant 1 cup ruby port

scant 1 cup heavy or whipping cream

1 tbsp confectioner's sugar

1 tsp vanilla extract

Preheat the oven to 350°F/180°C. Grease a 9-inch/23-cm shallow, square cake pan.

Place the chocolate and butter in a pan and heat gently, stirring, until melted. Remove from the heat and stir in the sugar.

Beat the eggs, vanilla extract, and ginger syrup into the chocolate mixture. Stir in the flour and chopped ginger, mixing evenly.

Pour the mixture into the prepared pan and bake for 30–35 minutes, until just firm to the touch.

Meanwhile, make the port cream. Place the port in a pan and simmer over medium-high heat until reduced to about 4 tbsp. Remove from the heat and let cool. Whip the cream until beginning to thicken, then beat in the sugar, reduced port, and vanilla, continuing to whip until it holds soft peaks.

Remove the brownies from the oven, let cool for 2–3 minutes in the pan, then cut into 8 triangles. Place on individual serving plates and add a spoonful of port cream to each. Top with pieces of candied ginger and serve warm.

cookie sheet treats

chocolate peanut butter bars

makes 25

10¹/₂ oz/300 g milk chocolate
2¹/₂ cups all-purpose flour
1 tsp baking powder
8 oz/225 g butter
1³/₄ cups brown sugar
2 cups rolled oats
¹/₂ cup chopped mixed nuts
1 egg, beaten
14 oz/400 g sweetened
condensed milk
¹/₃ cup crunchy peanut butter

Preheat the oven to 350°F/180°C. Finely chop the chocolate. Sift the flour and baking powder into a large bowl.

Add the butter to the flour and rub in until the mixture resembles bread crumbs. Stir in the sugar, oats, and chopped nuts.

Put a quarter of the mixture into a bowl and stir in the chopped chocolate. Set aside.

Stir the egg into the remaining mixture, then press into the bottom of a 12 x 8-inch/ 30 x 20-cm roasting pan.

Bake the base in the preheated oven for 15 minutes. Meanwhile, mix the condensed milk and peanut butter together. Pour the mixture over the base and spread evenly, then sprinkle the reserved chocolate mixture on top and press down lightly.

Return to the oven and bake for an additional 20 minutes, until golden brown. Let cool in the pan, then cut into bars or squares.

almond bars

makes 8
3 eggs
2/3 cup ground almonds
scant 1 1/2 cups milk powder
1 cup granulated sugar
1/2 tsp saffron threads
4 oz/115 g unsalted butter
1 tbsp slivered almonds

Preheat the oven to 325°F/160°C. Lightly beat the eggs together in a mixing bowl and set aside.

Place the ground almonds, milk powder, sugar, and saffron in a large mixing bowl and stir to mix well.

Melt the butter in a small pan over low heat. Pour the melted butter over the dry ingredients and mix well with a wooden spoon until thoroughly combined.

Add the beaten eggs to the mixture in the pan and stir to blend well.

Spread the mixture evenly in a shallow 8-inch/20-cm ovenproof dish, sprinkle with almonds and bake in the preheated oven for 45 minutes, or until a skewer inserted into the center comes out clean.

Remove from the oven and cut into bars or triangles. Serve hot or cold.

chocolate marshmallow fingers

makes 18

12 oz/350 g graham crackers

4^1/$_2$ oz/125 g semisweet chocolate, broken into pieces

8 oz/225 g butter

^{1}/$_8$ cup superfine sugar

2 tbsp unsweetened cocoa

2 tbsp honey

^{2}/$_3$ cup mini marshmallows

^{1}/$_2$ cup white chocolate chips

Put the graham crackers in a polythene bag and, using a rolling pin, crush into small pieces.

Put the chocolate, butter, sugar, cocoa, and honey in a pan and heat gently until melted. Remove from the heat and let cool slightly.

Stir the crushed crackers into the chocolate mixture until well mixed. Add the marshmallows and mix well then finally stir in the chocolate chips.

Turn the mixture into an 8-inch/20-cm square cake pan and lightly smooth the top. Put in the refrigerator and let chill for 2–3 hours, until set. Cut into fingers before serving.

macadamia nut caramel bars

makes 16

base

1 cup macadamia nuts

2 cups all-purpose flour

1 cup brown sugar

4 oz/115 g butter

topping

4 oz/115 g butter

$^1/_2$ cup brown sugar

1$^1/_2$ cups milk chocolate chips

Preheat the oven to 350°F/180°C. Halve the macadamia nuts. To make the base, whisk together the flour, sugar, and butter until the mixture resembles fine bread crumbs.

Press the mixture into the bottom of a 12 x 8-inch/30 x 20-cm jelly roll pan. Sprinkle over the nuts.

To make the topping, put the butter and sugar in a pan and, stirring constantly, slowly bring the mixture to a boil. Boil for 1 minute, stirring constantly, then carefully pour the mixture over the macadamia nuts.

Bake in the preheated oven for about 20 minutes, until the caramel topping is bubbling. Remove from the oven and immediately sprinkle the chocolate chips evenly on top. Leave for 2–3 minutes, until the chocolate chips start to melt, then, using the blade of a knife, swirl the chocolate over the top. Let cool in the pan, then cut into bars or squares.

hazelnut chocolate crunch

makes 12

4 oz/115 g unsalted butter,
plus extra for greasing
generous 2 cups rolled oats
1/3 cup hazelnuts, lightly toasted
and chopped
generous 1/3 cup all-purpose flour
scant 1/2 cup light
muscovado sugar
2 tbsp corn syrup
1/3 cup bittersweet
chocolate chips

Preheat the oven to 350°F/180°C. Grease a 9-inch/23-cm shallow, square baking pan. Mix the oats, nuts, and flour in a large bowl.

Place the butter, sugar, and syrup in a large pan and heat gently until the sugar has dissolved. Pour in the dry ingredients and mix well. Stir in the chocolate chips.

Turn the mixture into the prepared pan and bake in the preheated oven for 20–25 minutes, or until golden brown and firm to the touch. Using a knife, mark into bars or triangles and let cool in the pan. Cut the bars or triangles with a sharp knife before carefully removing them from the pan.

fruity bars

makes 14

sunflower or corn oil, for brushing

1¼ cups rolled oats

¾ cup raw sugar

½ cup raisins

4 oz/115 g lowfat sunflower
margarine, melted

Preheat the oven to 375°F/190°C. Lightly brush an 11 x 7-inch/28 x 18-cm shallow cake pan with oil. Combine the oats, sugar, and raisins with the margarine, stirring well.

Spoon the oat mixture into the pan and press down firmly with the back of a spoon. Bake in the preheated oven for 15–20 minutes, or until golden.

Using a sharp knife, score lines to mark out 14 bars, then let cool in the pan for 10 minutes. Carefully transfer the bars to a wire rack to cool completely.

caramel chocolate shortbread

makes 12

base

4 oz/115 g unsalted butter,
plus extra for greasing

scant 1 1/4 cups all-purpose flour

1/4 cup golden superfine sugar

filling and topping

7 oz/200 g butter

generous 1/2 cup golden
superfine sugar

3 tbsp corn syrup

14 fl oz/400 ml canned
sweetened condensed milk

7 squares bittersweet chocolate,
broken into pieces

Preheat the oven to 350°F/180°C. Grease a 9-inch/23-cm shallow square cake pan and line the bottom with parchment paper. Place the butter, flour, and sugar in a food processor and process until they begin to bind together. Press the mixture into the prepared pan and smooth the top. Bake in the preheated oven for 20–25 minutes, or until golden.

Meanwhile, make the filling. Place the butter, sugar, syrup, and condensed milk in a pan and heat gently until the sugar has dissolved. Bring to a boil and simmer for 6–8 minutes, stirring constantly, until the mixture becomes very thick. Remove the shortbread from the oven, then pour over the filling and chill in the refrigerator until firm.

To make the topping, melt the chocolate in a heatproof bowl set over a pan of gently simmering water. Remove from the heat and let cool slightly, then spread over the caramel. Chill in the refrigerator until set. Cut it into 12 pieces with a sharp knife and serve.

cinnamon squares

makes 12

8 oz/225 g butter, softened, plus
extra for greasing
1 1/4 cups superfine sugar
3 eggs, beaten lightly
1 3/4 cups self-rising flour
1/2 tsp baking soda
1 tbsp ground cinnamon
2/3 cup sour cream
1/2 cup sunflower seeds

Preheat the oven to 350°F/180°C. Grease a 9-inch/23-cm square cake pan with a little butter and line the bottom with baking parchment.

In a large mixing bowl, cream together the butter and superfine sugar until the mixture is light and fluffy.

Gradually add the beaten eggs to the mixture, beating thoroughly after each addition.

Sift the flour, baking soda, and cinnamon together into the creamed mixture and fold in, using a metal spoon in a figure-of-eight movement.

Spoon in the sour cream and sunflower seeds and mix gently until well combined.

Spoon the mixture into the prepared cake pan and smooth the surface with the back of a spoon or a knife.

Bake in the preheated oven for about 45 minutes, until the mixture is firm to the touch when pressed with a finger.

Loosen the edges with a round-bladed knife, then turn out onto a wire rack to cool completely. Slice into 12 squares before serving.

chocolate peppermint bars

serves 16

4 oz/115 g unsalted butter,
plus extra for greasing
$^1/_2$ cup superfine sugar
generous 1$^1/_3$ cups
all-purpose flour
2$^1/_2$ cups confectioners' sugar
2–4 tbsp warm water
1 tsp peppermint extract
few drops of green food
coloring (optional)
12 squares bittersweet chocolate,
broken into pieces

Preheat the oven to 350°F/180°C. Grease a 12 x 8-inch/30 x 20-cm jelly roll pan and line with baking parchment. Beat the butter and sugar together until pale and fluffy. Stir in the flour until the mixture binds together.

Knead the mixture to form a smooth dough, then press into the prepared pan. Prick the surface all over with a fork. Bake in the preheated oven for 10–15 minutes, or until lightly browned and just firm to the touch. Remove from the oven and let cool in the pan.

Sift the confectioners' sugar into a bowl. Gradually add the water, then add the peppermint extract and food coloring if using. Spread the frosting over the base, then let set.

Melt the chocolate in a heatproof bowl set over a pan of gently simmering water, then remove from the heat and spread over the frosting. Let set, then cut into slices.

nutty granola squares

makes 16

4 oz/115 g unsalted butter, plus
extra for greasing
4 tbsp honey
1/8 cup unrefined superfine sugar
scant 3 cups rolled oats
generous 1/8 cup dried cranberries
generous 1/8 cup pitted dates,
chopped
generous 1/8 cup hazelnuts,
chopped
5/8 cup slivered almonds

Preheat the oven to 375°F/190°C. Grease an 8-inch/20-cm square baking pan.

Melt the butter with the honey and sugar in a pan and stir together. Add the remaining ingredients and mix thoroughly.

Turn the mixture into the prepared pan and press down well. Bake in the preheated oven for 20–30 minutes.

Remove from the oven and let cool in the pan. Cut into 16 squares.

strawberry & chocolate bars

makes 16

1¹/2 cups all-purpose flour

1 tsp baking powder

¹/2 cup superfine sugar

scant ¹/2 cup soft brown sugar

8 oz/225 g unsalted butter

1 cup rolled oats

²/3 cup strawberry preserve

scant ²/3 cup semisweet
chocolate chips

scant ¹/4 cup slivered almonds,
flaked

Preheat the oven to 375°F/190°C. Line a 12 x 8-inch/30 x 20-cm deep-sided jelly roll pan with baking parchment. Sift the flour and baking powder into a large bowl.

Add the superfine sugar and brown sugar to the flour and mix well. Add the butter and rub in until the mixture resembles bread crumbs. Stir in the rolled oats.

Press three-fourths of the mixture into the bottom of the prepared cake pan. Bake in the preheated oven for 10 minutes.

Spread the preserve over the cooked base, then sprinkle over the chocolate chips. Mix the remaining flour mixture with the almonds. Sprinkle evenly over the chocolate chips and press down gently.

Return to the oven and bake for an additional 20–25 minutes, or until golden brown. Remove from the oven and let cool in the pan, then cut into bars.